HOW TO BE REASONABLE

REASONABLE

REASONABLE

REASONABLE

REASONABLE

REASONABLE

SKEPTICAL

REASONABLE

DON'T WORRY ABOUT THAT WORD, IT'LL COME UP LATER.

HYPATIA
PRESS

Published by Hypatia Press in the United Kingdom

ISBN 978-1-910780-76-3

Cover design by Rebecca Fox

www.hypatiapress.org

HOW TO BE REASONABLE

BY SOMEONE WHO TRIED EVERYTHING ELSE

REBECCA FOX

JUST TO MAKE SURE
WE'RE ON THE SAME PAGE,
THE DEFINITION OF REASONABLE
I'M PARTIAL TO IS:

'AGREEING TO THE RULES OF LOGIC
AND FOLLOWING EVIDENCE.'

OH, AND ALSO:

'SENSIBLE, FAIR AND OPEN MINDED.'

SOUNDS PRETTY GOOD,
RIGHT?

HOWTOBEREASONABLE.COM

THIS IS ME.
I AM SURROUNDED BY ALL THE STUFF AND NONSENSE IN THE WORLD. WE ALL ARE.
HAPPY 21ST
I DIDN'T HAVE ANY RELIABLE METHOD TO DETERMINE WHICH WAS WHICH. SO, LIKE MOST OF US, I USED A RAMSHACKLE COLLECTION OF INTUITIONS, BIASES AND DESIRES TO DECIDE WHAT TO BELIEVE.[1]
I WANT TO BELIEVE
WE USE OUR BELIEFS TO INFORM THE DECISIONS WE MAKE. IF OUR BELIEFS ARE INACCURATE THE DECISIONS WE MAKE BASED ON THEM CAN BE DANGEROUS.
I NEVER GOT BADLY HURT, BUT MANY PEOPLE DO.[2]
I HAD AMASSED A LOT OF BELIEFS. SOME OF THEM CONTRADICTED EACH OTHER, OTHERS CONFUSED ME IF I THOUGHT ABOUT THEM TOO DEEPLY. SO I DIDN'T...
CHARIOTS OF THE GODS
...UNTIL I HAD TO.

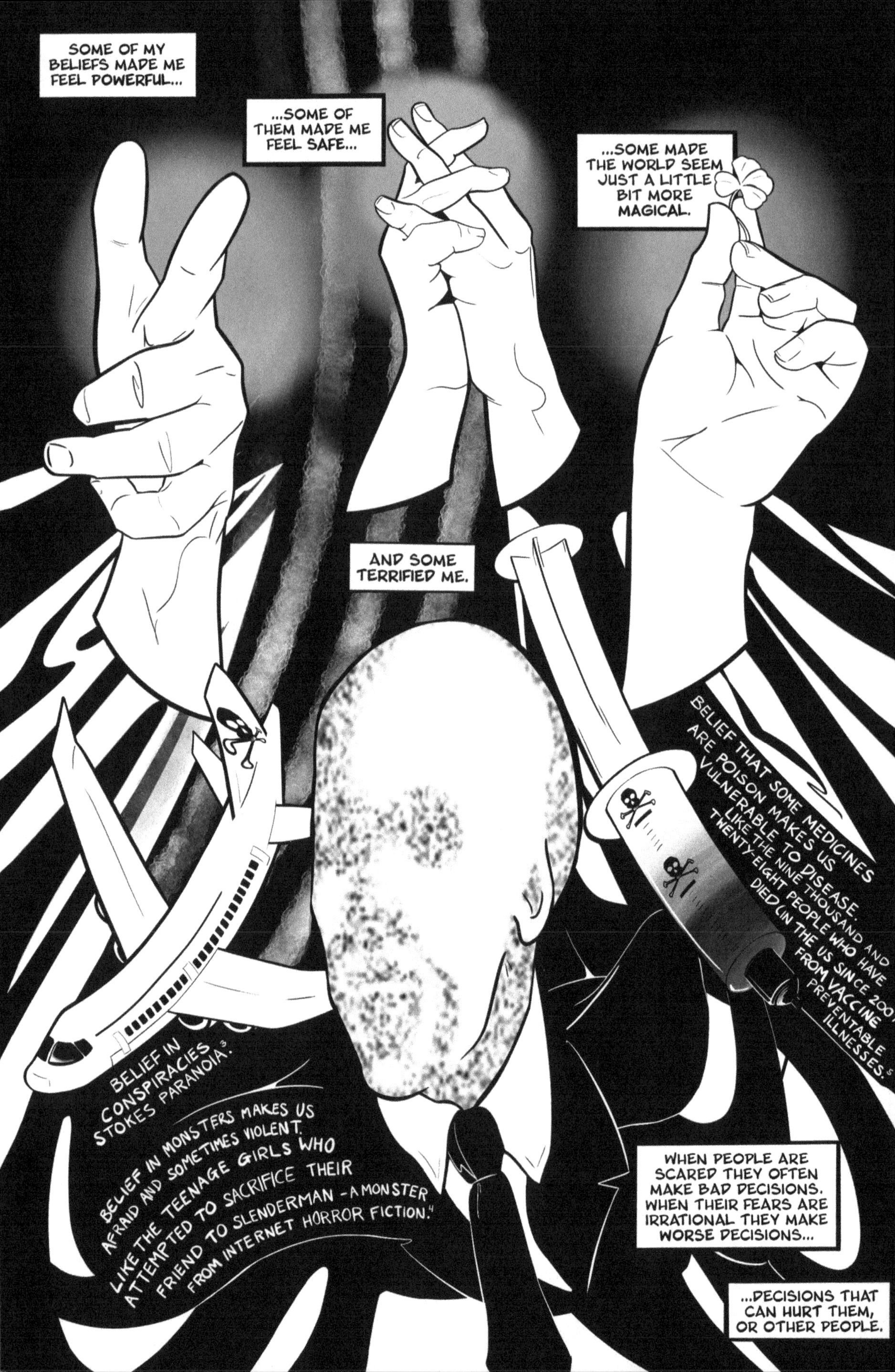
SOME OF MY BELIEFS MADE ME FEEL POWERFUL...
...SOME OF THEM MADE ME FEEL SAFE...
...SOME MADE THE WORLD SEEM JUST A LITTLE BIT MORE MAGICAL.
AND SOME TERRIFIED ME.
BELIEF THAT SOME MEDICINES ARE POISON MAKES US VULNERABLE TO DISEASE.
LIKE THE NINE THOUSAND AND TWENTY-EIGHT PEOPLE WHO HAVE DIED (IN THE US SINCE 2007
FROM VACCINE PREVENTABLE ILLNESSES.[5]
BELIEF IN CONSPIRACIES STOKES PARANOIA.[3]
BELIEF IN MONSTERS MAKES US AFRAID AND SOMETIMES VIOLENT.
LIKE THE TEENAGE GIRLS WHO ATTEMPTED TO SACRIFICE THEIR FRIEND TO SLENDERMAN - A MONSTER FROM INTERNET HORROR FICTION.[4]
WHEN PEOPLE ARE SCARED THEY OFTEN MAKE BAD DECISIONS. WHEN THEIR FEARS ARE IRRATIONAL THEY MAKE WORSE DECISIONS...
...DECISIONS THAT CAN HURT THEM, OR OTHER PEOPLE.

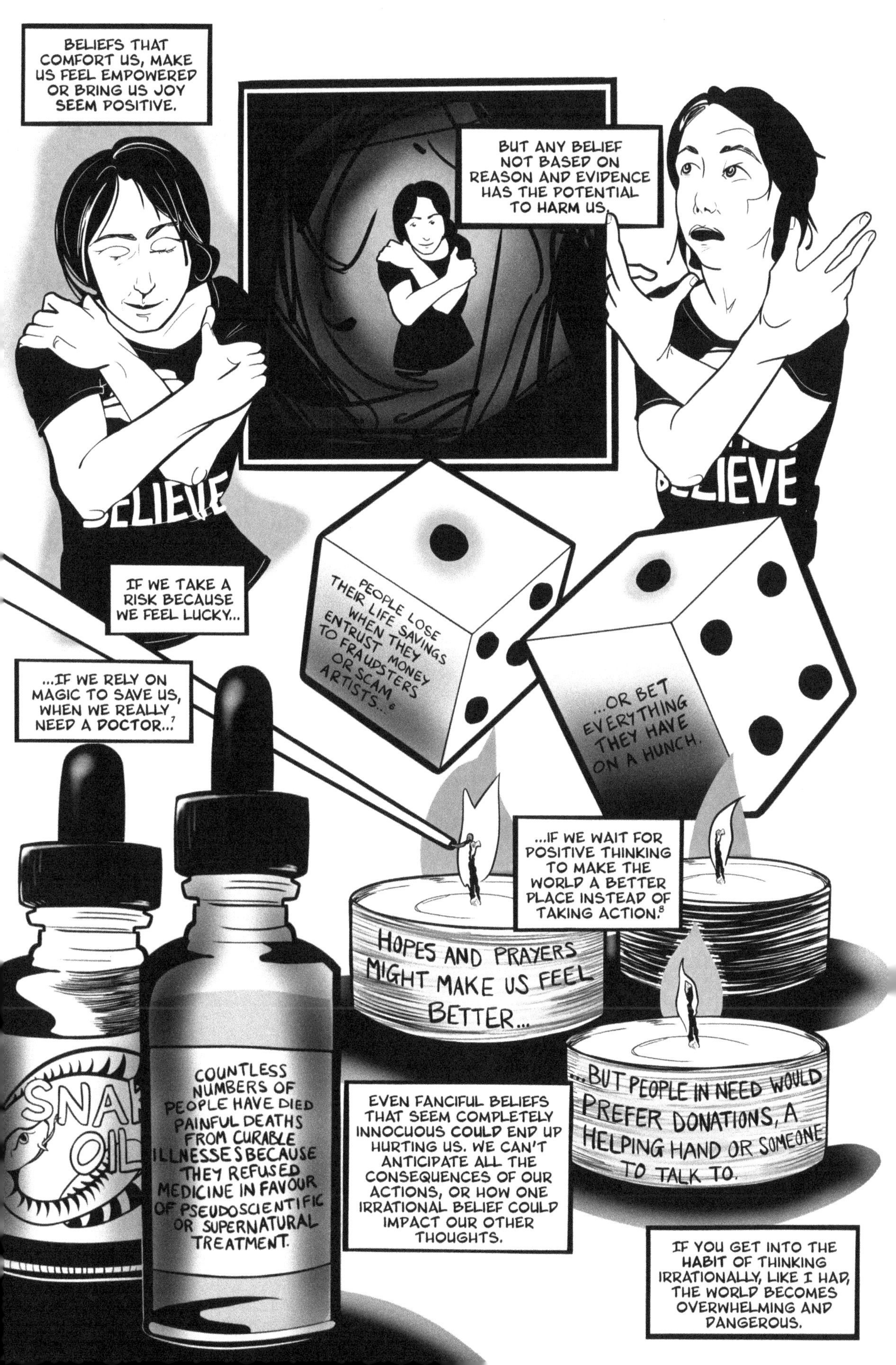
BELIEFS THAT COMFORT US, MAKE US FEEL EMPOWERED OR BRING US JOY SEEM POSITIVE.
BUT ANY BELIEF NOT BASED ON REASON AND EVIDENCE HAS THE POTENTIAL TO HARM US.
BELIEVE
BELIEVE
IF WE TAKE A RISK BECAUSE WE FEEL LUCKY...
PEOPLE LOSE THEIR LIFE SAVINGS WHEN THEY ENTRUST MONEY TO FRAUDSTERS OR SCAM ARTISTS...[6]
...OR BET EVERYTHING THEY HAVE ON A HUNCH.
...IF WE RELY ON MAGIC TO SAVE US, WHEN WE REALLY NEED A DOCTOR...[7]
...IF WE WAIT FOR POSITIVE THINKING TO MAKE THE WORLD A BETTER PLACE INSTEAD OF TAKING ACTION.[8]
HOPES AND PRAYERS MIGHT MAKE US FEEL BETTER...
...BUT PEOPLE IN NEED WOULD PREFER DONATIONS, A HELPING HAND OR SOMEONE TO TALK TO.
COUNTLESS NUMBERS OF PEOPLE HAVE DIED PAINFUL DEATHS FROM CURABLE ILLNESSES BECAUSE THEY REFUSED MEDICINE IN FAVOUR OF PSEUDOSCIENTIFIC OR SUPERNATURAL TREATMENT.
EVEN FANCIFUL BELIEFS THAT SEEM COMPLETELY INNOCUOUS COULD END UP HURTING US. WE CAN'T ANTICIPATE ALL THE CONSEQUENCES OF OUR ACTIONS, OR HOW ONE IRRATIONAL BELIEF COULD IMPACT OUR OTHER THOUGHTS.
IF YOU GET INTO THE HABIT OF THINKING IRRATIONALLY, LIKE I HAD, THE WORLD BECOMES OVERWHELMING AND DANGEROUS.

EVENTUALLY I WAS FEELING SO LOST AND ANXIOUS I REALISED I HAD TO RECONSIDER MY BELIEFS.
WHEN I STARTED LOOKING, I FOUND PEOPLE WHO HAD EXAMINED AND EVALUATED THE IDEAS I HELD DEAR.
MAYBE THEY WERE RIGHT, MAYBE THEY WERE WRONG. BUT IN MY RESEARCH I FOUND SOMETHING I WASN'T LOOKING FOR...
I WANT TO BELIEVE
...THESE PEOPLE HAD A METHOD FOR DISCERNING TRUTH–AND I NEEDED ONE.
CARL SAGAN
THE METHOD IS, SIMPLY, BEING REASONABLE: PRIORITISING REASON AND EVIDENCE WHILE TRYING TO REMAIN FAIR AND OPEN-MINDED. THEY CALL THEMSELVES SKEPTICS, PERHAPS BECAUSE 'REASONABLISTS' IS TOO MUCH OF A MOUTHFUL.[9]
I WANT TO BELIEVE
THIS COMIC IS A SHORT INTRODUCTION TO SCIENTIFIC SKEPTICISM FOR PEOPLE WHO ARE LOST AND CONFUSED, OR WHO JUST WANT TO IMPROVE THEIR CRITICAL THINKING SKILLS AND BECOME A BIT MORE REASONABLE

THE TORRENT OF STUFF AND NONSENSE HASN'T GONE AWAY.

OVER 1 BILLION WEBSITES

NEARLY 130 MILLION BOOKS

I WANT TO BELIEVE

IN FACT, IF ANYTHING IT NOW SEEMS FASTER, WIDER AND MORE TURBULENT.

BUT NOW, AS I WADE THROUGH IT, I AM GUIDED BY THE SIX PRINCIPLES OF SKEPTICISM WHICH HELP ME KEEP MY BALANCE.

C RI SITY

H M LITY

QUE ST ONING

INTRO SPECTION

EXTROSPECTIO

ACTION

YOU DON'T NEED TO PEER AROUND MY LEGS! I'LL GO INTO MORE DETAIL ON THE SIX PRINCIPLES OVER THE NEXT FEW PAGES

PRINCIPLE 1:
CURIOSITY
CURIOSITY IS WHAT DRIVES HUMANITY FORWARD.
IF WE WEREN'T CURIOUS WE WOULD NEVER ASK QUESTIONS LIKE...
...IS THIS RIGHT?...
...COULD WE DO THIS A BETTER WAY?
I WANT TO BELIEVE
AND ALL PROGRESS- MORAL, SCIENTIFIC AND ARTISTIC- WOULD CEASE.
SKEPTICISM, LIKE SCIENCE, IS DRIVEN BY CURIOSITY. THE BASIC QUESTION...
... I WONDER IF THAT'S TRUE?..
...PROMPTS AND SUSTAINS SKEPTICAL INQUIRY.

PRINCIPLE 2:
HUMILITY
UNKNOWN UNKNOWNS
KNOWN UNKNOWNS
THINGS HUMANITY KNOWS
THINGS I KNOW*
BEING ABLE TO ADMIT YOU DON'T KNOW SOMETHING IS THE FIRST STEP TO DISCOVERY...
...AND YOU BETTER GET USED TO IT, BECAUSE THERE'S A WHOLE LOT OF STUFF THAT WE DON'T KNOW.
I WANT TO BELIEVE
*NOT TO SCALE
OUR CULTURE PRIZES STEADFAST AND DECISIVE PEOPLE, BUT A SKEPTIC WOULD RATHER BE CAUTIOUS AND OPEN TO CHANGING THEIR MIND.

PRINCIPLE 3:
QUESTIONING
SKEPTICS ARE LIKE TODDLERS, OUR FAVOURITE PUNCTUATION IS THE QUESTION MARK.
WHERE?
WHO?
WHAT?
WHY?
MY TREASURED BELIEF
WHO?
WE WANT TO KNOW WHY PEOPLE BELIEVE WHAT THEY DO, HOW THINGS WORK AND IN GENERAL...
...WHAT'S GOING ON?
WHERE?
UNLIKE TODDLERS WE WILL NOT ACCEPT THE ANSWER 'BECAUSE I SAID SO'...
MY IMPERFECT BRAIN
...SO DON'T EVEN TRY!

PRINCIPLE 4:
INTROSPECTION
SKEPTICS ARE ON A NEVER ENDING QUEST TO BECOME MORE AWARE OF OUR OWN MOTIVATIONS AND BIASES.
WE REALISE THAT HUMAN BRAINS ARE PRONE TO ALL SORTS OF BIASES, MISPERCEPTIONS AND CONFUSIONS.[10]
SO WE TRY TO BE MINDFUL OF THE MISTAKES WE'RE MAKING AND GUARD AGAINST LETTING THEM HAMPER OUR CRITICAL THINKING SKILLS.
SPOTTING OUR OWN BIASES IS CHALLENGING, BUT WE DON'T HAVE TO DO IT ALONE.
I'M WITH BIASED
I WANT TO
I'M WITH BIASED
WE CAN RELY ON OUR FRIENDS, FAMILY AND FELLOW SKEPTICS TO HELP US FOCUS OUR INTROSPECTION...
... TO POINT OUT OUR BLIND SPOTS AND RESPECTFULLY REMIND US OF OUR BIASES.

PRINCIPLE 5:
EXTROSPECTION
SKEPTICS USE THE SCIENTIFIC METHOD TO INVESTIGATE THE NATURAL WORLD. THIS MEANS WE OBSERVE THE WORLD, COME UP WITH IDEAS, THEN TEST THEM.
YES, THAT'S A REAL WORD! IT'S THE OPPOSITE OF INTROSPECTION (LOOKING AT THE WORLD AROUND YOU, INSTEAD OF THE WORLD INSIDE YOU). STOP BEING SO SKEPTICAL!
HUMANS EXPLORING MY HOME HAVE FOUND CURES FOR MANY DISEASES.[12]
BUT I WISH THEY'D BE A LITTLE MORE CAREFUL.
WE WANT TO KNOW HOW OUR UNIVERSE WORKS BECAUSE IT'S MORE FASCINATING AND BEAUTIFUL THE MORE WE KNOW ABOUT IT...
QUININE (TREATS MALARIA)
GALANTAMINE (TREATS ALZHEIMER'S)
ASPRIN
D-TUBOCURARINE (TOXIN THAT ACTS AS A MUSCLE RELAXANT)
...AND BECAUSE KNOWING HOW THE WORLD WORKS MAKES US BETTER AT LIVING IN IT.
VINBLASTINE + VINCRISTINE (TREAT LEUKAEMIA + HODGKIN'S LYMPHOMA)
THE SCIENTIFIC METHOD HAS HELPED US DEVELOP DROUGHT RESISTANT CROPS TO FEED HUNGRY PEOPLE.[13]
OH YEAH, AND IT GOT US INTO SPACE!
WE USE THE SCIENTIFIC METHOD BECAUSE IT IS THE MOST RELIABLE, OBJECTIVE AND EFFICACIOUS SYSTEM HUMANITY HAS SO FAR DISCOVERED FOR UNDERSTANDING OUR WORLD.
IN OTHER WORDS, BECAUSE IT WORKS.

PRINCIPLE 6:
A SKEPTIC ASPIRES TO ALIGN THEIR BELIEFS WITH EVIDENCE AND THEIR BEHAVIOUR WITH THEIR BELIEFS.
ACTION
TRUTH
HEART
I ♥ VENN DIAGRAMS
WHERE SKEPTICS LIVE
THE SKEPTICAL MOVEMENT IS COMPRISED OF PEOPLE WHO CARE ABOUT THE TRUTH AND ABOUT OTHER PEOPLE.[14]
WE ARE ALL TRYING TO MAKE A DIFFERENCE IN OUR OWN WAY.
DOWN WITH THIS SORT OF THING
SKEPTICS ARE CONCERNED THAT PEOPLE PUT THEMSELVES AND OTHERS AT RISK BY MAKING DECISIONS BASED ON A MISUNDERSTANDING OF THE WORLD.
SO THEY TAKE ACTION BY TRYING TO EDUCATE PEOPLE AND PROTECT THEM FROM MAKING DANGEROUS MISTAKES![15]

BUT MAYBE THE MOST IMPORTANT OF THESE PRINCIPLES ARE THE FIRST TWO...
CURIOSITY & HUMILITY
THEY ARE THE EASIEST AND HARDEST OF THEM ALL.
WHAT HAPPENS WHEN A CATERPILLAR GOES INTO A CHRYSALIS?
IT TURNS INTO A BUTTERFLY? ...OR A MOTH?
YEAH, BUT HOW?
SOMETHING LIKE THIS...?
WE WANT TO KNOW THE TRUTH, BUT OUR BRAINS ARE QUICK TO CONFABULATE ANSWERS WHICH WE STUBBORNLY INSIST ARE TRUE.
ARE YOU SURE?
UMMM... NO?
THEN THOSE ANSWERS DAMPEN OUR CURIOSITY AND WE NEVER FIND OUT THE TRUTH.[16]
A SKEPTIC SHOULD BE PROUD TO DECLARE...
I DON'T KNOW!
BECAUSE (AT LEAST FOR ME) IT'S USUALLY TRUE, AND IT'S THE FIRST STEP TO DISCOVERING SOMETHING NEW.
DON'T WORRY, I'LL GET BACK TO THE CATERPILLAR LATER.

THAT WOULD BE THE END OF THE COMIC IF ONLY OUR BRAINS WERE PERFECTLY REASONABLE ORGANS, BUT THEY'RE NOT.
OUR BRAINS MAKE MISTAKES.
WHEN YOU LET DOWN YOUR GUARD...
HA!
YOUR SILLY BRAIN LEADS YOU ASTRAY...
AND YOU MAKE A MISTAKE.
I WANT TO BELIEVE
TO UNDERSTAND THE WORLD WE NEED TO BE AWARE OF THE COMMON MALFUNCTIONS THAT THIS EQUIPMENT BETWEEN OUR EARS IS SUSCEPTIBLE TO.
TO DO THAT I SUGGEST SOMEWHERE ON YOUR BODY YOU TATTOO THESE FIVE WORDS: DON'T BELIEVE EVERYTHING YOU THINK.
Don't believe Everything you think
THE LAMP POST MIGHT REPRESENT TOO-GOOD-TO-BE-TRUE POLITICAL PROMISES, HANDSOME (BUT BAD) MEN, ANYTHING FOR FREE, NIGERIAN PRINCES, SNAKE OIL, SCARY STORIES ABOUT CHEMICALS OR GHOSTS, CONSPIRACY THEORIES, UFO's, PROPAGHANDHA, ANTI-SCIENCE RHETORIC, SCIENTOLOGY, PEOPLE WHO CLAIM TO KNOW THE FUTURE OR TALK TO THE DEAD, SCAMS, HOAXES, UNSUBSTANTIATED CLAIMS ABOUT HISTORY...ON THE HISTORY CHANNEL! LUCKY CHARMS OR TRINKETS, PSYCHIC SURGERY - 'PSYCHIC' ANYTHING! MISOGYNY OR RACISM POSING AS 'SCIENCE', CHIROPRACTIC, GET-RICH-QUICK SCHEMES, COLD FUSION DEVICES, BIGFOOT, AND OF COURSE - MOTHMAN!
OH NO! NOT INTROSPECTION!
IF A TATTOO SEEMS TOO EXTREME AT LEAST COMMIT YOURSELF TO LEARNING ABOUT THE COGNITIVE BIASES, LOGICAL FALLACIES AND WISHFUL THINKING THAT GOES ON IN ALL OF OUR HEADS![17]
OVER THE NEXT FEW PAGES I'LL INTRODUCE YOU TO THE BIGGEST CULPRITS.

COMMON BRAIN MISTAKES 1:

CONFIRMATION BIAS

AN UNFORTUNATE SIDE EFFECT IS THAT CONFIRMATION BIAS PROTECTS AND PERPETUATES INACCURATE IDEAS, LIKE 'BLACK CATS ARE UNLUCKY'. AND MANY MORE DANGEROUS BELIEFS![18]

COMMON BRAIN MISTAKES 2:
THE HALO EFFECT AND AD HOMINEM ARGUMENTS
THE HALO EFFECT IS OUR BRAIN'S HABIT OF ASSUMING ONE TRAIT IS REPRESENTATIVE OF A WHOLE PERSON, GROUP OR THING.
WHEN WE NOTICE A SINGLE NEGATIVE THING ABOUT A PERSON, PRODUCT OR PLACE WE THINK WE HAVE UNDERSTOOD EVERYTHING ABOUT THAT PERSON OR THING.
AND, IF WE HEAR ONLY ONE GOOD THING ABOUT A PERSON WE ASSUME THEY ARE A SAINT.
WHAT A KOOKY WEIRDO!
THIS IS WHY AD HOMINEM ARGUMENTS, DIRECTED AGAINST A PERSON'S CHARACTER RATHER THAN THEIR IDEAS, WORK SO WELL...
WHAT A NICE MAN!
LET'S TRY SOME VEGGIE FOOD!
...AND CAN BE SO MISLEADING.[19]
LET'S GO TO WAR!
BUT THAT'S HIPPY FOOD!
NO THANKS!
WELL IF MEN IN SUITS SAY SO...
...UH, OKAY?
THE PERSONALITY OR HISTORY OF A PERSON PROMOTING AN IDEA MIGHT GIVE YOU AN INDICATION WHETHER IT SHOULD BE TAKEN SERIOUSLY. BUT YOU SHOULD NEVER ACCEPT OR DISMISS AN IDEA BASED ON THE QUIRKS OF ITS PROPONENTS.

COMMON BRAIN MISTAKES 3:

PROBABILITY IS CONFUSING

COMMON BRAIN MISTAKES 4:
THE IDENTIFIABLE VICTIM EFFECT
DOG SHELTER
POOR ABANDONED PUPPIES NEED BISCUITS AND CUDDLES
KIDS HOSPIT
ADORABLE KIDS WITH VERY RARE DISEASES NEED BANDAGES AND TOYS
WE RESPOND MUCH MORE EMPATHETICALLY TO THE STORY OF ONE INDIVIDUAL'S STRUGGLE THAN WE DO TO THE SUFFERING OF MILLIONS.
THAT'S WHY CHARITIES TELL THE STORIES OF INDIVIDUALS INSTEAD OF DRY FACTS.
THOSE POSTERS ARE CONSIDERABLY MORE COMPELLING THAN THESE NUMBERS:
OVER 56 BILLION LAND ANIMALS ARE KILLED EVERY YEAR.[22]
OVER 1 MILLION PEOPLE DIE FROM MALARIA EVERY YEAR.[23]
MOSTLY CHICKENS
BUT, IF WE CARE ABOUT THE SUFFERING OF ANIMALS OR THE RAVAGES OF DISEASE THEN THE NUMBERS SHOULD HORRIFY US MUCH MORE.
AND THE NUMBERS SHOULD INFORM OUR DECISIONS ABOUT WHICH CAUSES WE FOCUS OUR EFFORTS ON.[24]
IF WE WANT TO MAKE THE WORLD A BETTER PLACE WE WILL NEED EMPATHY... AND MATHS.[25]
RIP

COMMON BRAIN MISTAKES 5:
APPEAL TO NATURE
HAVE YOU EVER PAID EXTRA FOR SOMETHING LABELED 'ALL NATURAL', EXCUSED BEHAVIOUR BECAUSE IT'S 'ONLY NATURAL', OR BEEN RELIEVED TO HEAR THAT SOMETHING IS 'NATURALLY SOURCED'?
I CERTAINLY HAVE.
THAT'S BECAUSE WHEN WE HEAR 'NATURAL' WE MISTAKENLY ASSUME IT MEANS 'GOOD'.
IN FACT 'NATURAL' IS A DIFFICULT WORD TO PIN DOWN. DOES IT MEAN THAT SOMETHING GREW THAT WAY? HAS BEEN THAT WAY SINCE FOREVER? OR THAT IT HAS NEVER BEEN TOUCHED BY HUMAN HANDS?
MODERN MEDICINE
STINGING NETTLES
MAYBE IT JUST MEANS THAT THERE ARE NO CHEMICALS IN IT...? BUT THEN, EVERYTHING IS COMPOSED OF CHEMICALS SO IF THAT'S OUR DEFINITION NOTHING CAN BE NATURAL.
HERPES
CULTIVATED BANANA
EVEN IF WE GET A CLEAR DEFINITION OF THE WORD 'NATURAL' (MAYBE SOMETHING LIKE: 'EXISTS FREE FROM HUMAN INTERVENTION'), THE IDEA THAT NATURAL = GOOD IS STILL FLAWED.
BECAUSE, IF YOU THINK ABOUT IT, NOT EVERYTHING THAT OCCURS IN NATURE IS GOOD. IN FACT SOME NATURAL THINGS ARE REALLY, REALLY BAD.
SO SOMETHING MIGHT BE 'NATURAL' AND GOOD BUT NOTHING IS GOOD BECAUSE IT IS 'NATURAL'.
SIMILARLY SOMETHING MAY BE 'UNNATURAL' AND BAD BUT NOTHING IS BAD BECAUSE IT IS 'UNNATURAL'.

COMMON BRAIN MISTAKES 6:
FASHIONABLE THINKING AND ANECDOTAL EVIDENCE
HUMANS ARE SOCIAL CREATURES. WE TEND TO GO ALONG WITH WHAT OTHER PEOPLE DO AND THINK. THAT'S USUALLY OKAY, IN FACT IT CAN BE HELPFUL. IF EVERYONE'S RAVING ABOUT A NEW RESTAURANT MAYBE YOU SHOULD GO AND CHECK IT OUT...
IF EVERYONE WALKED OFF A CLIFF WOULD YOU?
I MEAN, YEAH, PROBABLY...
...BUT ASSUMING THAT SOMETHING IS TRUE JUST BECAUSE EVERYONE SAYS SO IS A MISTAKE.[26]
ANOTHER MISTAKE WE CAN MAKE BECAUSE WE ARE SOCIAL AND NARRATIVE LOVING CREATURES IS RELYING ON ANECDOTAL EVIDENCE.
AN ANECDOTE FROM OUR FRIEND ABOUT HOW GREAT SOMETHING IS SEEMS MORE CONVINCING THAN A BORING LIST OF DATA OR A SCIENTIFIC STUDY - WHEN IN FACT THE LATTER IS MUCH MORE LIKELY TO BE ACCURATE.
...TO SURVIVE, THE BIGFOOT 'BREEDING POPULATION' MUST BE AT LEAST 100,000 IN NORTH AMERICA. AND YET, NO SAMPLE OF BIGFOOT D.N.A. HAS EVER BEEN FOUND...[27]
BORING ECOLOGIST PHD TYPE
UH HUH.
I WANT TO
RAKISH UNCLE BOB
WOW!
I WANT TO
ANECDOTES, NO MATTER HOW COMPELLING, SHOULD NOT OVERRULE DATA.

THE BRAIN MISTAKES I'VE LISTED OVER THE LAST FEW PAGES ARE JUST THE ONES MY BRAIN MAKES MOST FREQUENTLY. THERE ARE MANY MORE TO BE ON GUARD FOR.
IF YOU HAVE NEVER EXPERIENCED ANY OF THESE MISTAKES THEN YOU MUST BE SOME KIND OF MAGICAL CLEVER PIXIE- CONGRATULATIONS.
I WANT TO BELIEVE
JUST KIDDING! IF YOU THINK YOU HAVE NEVER EXPERIENCED ANY OF THESE MISTAKES, YOU'RE PROBABLY SUFFERING FROM THE MOST INSIDIOUS BIAS OF ALL...
IMMUNITY BIAS
BECAUSE IT'S SO MUCH HARDER TO SPOT OUR OWN BIASES THAN IT IS TO SPOT OTHER PEOPLE'S WE CAN EASILY DELUDE OURSELVES INTO THINKING WE ARE IMMUNE.
WAIT, WHAT?
IF YOU CONSIDER YOURSELF A REASONABLE PERSON, OR A SKEPTIC (OR BOTH) IT'S EVEN MORE TEMPTING TO THINK THAT YOU HAVE CONQUERED THEM ALL...
I WANT TO BELIEVE
...BUT YOU NEVER WILL. WE CAN BECOME MORE AWARE OF THE MISTAKES OUR BRAINS MAKE BUT WE WILL NEVER ELIMINATE THEM ENTIRELY.
THE ONLY WAY TO DEAL WITH THEM IS TO TRY AND THINK CAREFULLY ABOUT WHAT MISTAKES WE COULD BE MAKING AND TO CREATE COMMUNITIES THAT CHALLENGE US IN RESPECTFUL,HELPFUL WAYS.

OF COURSE, THE HARDEST TIME TO SPOT YOUR OWN BIASES OR MISTAKES IS WHEN YOU WANT TO BELIEVE.
DAMNIT! I ALREADY BOUGHT THE T-SHIRT
WHEN YOU ARE REALLY ATTACHED TO AN IDEA IS WHEN YOU HAVE TO BE MOST CAREFUL.
IF YOU'RE EMOTIONALLY, SOCIALLY OR FINANCIALLY INVESTED IT'S EVEN HARDER.[28]

I WANT TO BELIEVE
THERE MUST BE SOMETHING OUT THERE.
WE ARE ALL PART ALIEN... BUT SOME MORE THAN OTHERS.
BETTER SAFE THAN SORRY!
I WANT TO BELIEVE
I WANT TO BELIEVE
TIN FOIL HATS 3 FOR £10
EMOTIONAL INVESTMENT
FINANCIAL INVESTMENT
IDENTITY INVESTMENT
IT'S IMPORTANT TO TAKE YOUR MOST TREASURED BELIEFS OUT OF THEIR GLASS CABINETS AND ENSURE THEY ARE FALSIFIABLE. TO SAY A BELIEF IS FALSIFIABLE MEANS THAT IT'S POSSIBLE THAT THE BELIEF COULD BE TESTED AND PROVEN FALSE.[29]
AN IDEA THAT CAN'T BE TESTED CAN'T TELL US ANYTHING ABOUT REALITY, BECAUSE THE WORLD IN WHICH THE BELIEF IS TRUE LOOKS EXACTLY LIKE THE WORLD IN WHICH IT IS FALSE.
UNFALSIFIABLE IDEAS MAY BE APPROPRIATE IN THE REALM OF ART AND ENTERTAINMENT, BUT THEY SHOULD NOT BE INFORMING YOUR IMPORTANT DECISIONS.

A FALSIFIABILITY EXERCISE

RESEARCH SKILLS
ONCE YOU'VE GOT THAT BELIEF IN YOUR MIND, AND WRITTEN THE TWO SENTENCES, YOU HAVE SET YOURSELF A SMALL RESEARCH PROJECT.
LET'S GET STARTED!
TO COMPLETE THIS RESEARCH PROJECT YOU WILL NEED NINE BASIC RESEARCH SKILLS.
1
DISREGARD ANECDOTES
WHEN WE BEGIN RESEARCHING A SUBJECT OUR IMMEDIATE INSTINCT IS TO ASK PEOPLE WHO'VE HAD FIRST HAND EXPERIENCE.
BUT PEOPLE'S EXPERIENCES ARE SUBJECTIVE, LIABLE TO BE BIASED AND PERHAPS MISREPRESENTATIVE.
ANECDOTES CAN INSPIRE AND INTEREST US BUT THEY CAN'T BE A SUBSTITUTE FOR EVIDENCE.
NOT TODAY AUNT MARTHA!
2
READ THE WIKI
WIKIPEDIA
A GOOD PLACE TO START IS WIKIPEDIA...[30]
I'M NOT SAYING YOUR RESEARCH SHOULD BEGIN AND END THERE BUT IT WILL GIVE YOU AN OVERVIEW OF THE SORT OF THINGS YOU NEED TO LOOK INTO.
WIKIPEDIA IS GREAT BECAUSE YOU CAN CHECK THE SOURCES OF THE INFORMATION YOURSELF - THEY DON'T EXPECT YOU TO TAKE THEIR WORD FOR ANYTHING.

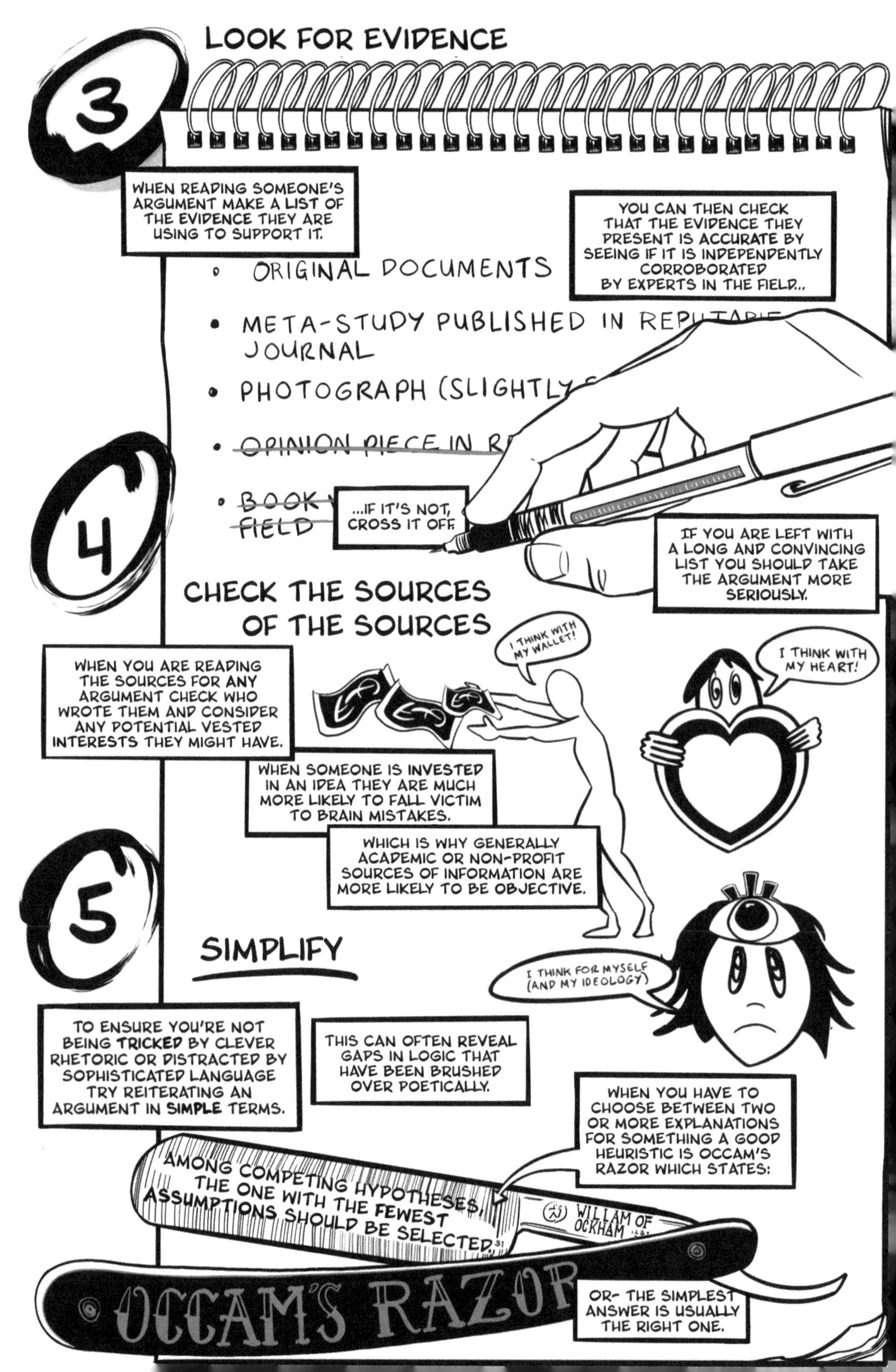
3
LOOK FOR EVIDENCE
WHEN READING SOMEONE'S ARGUMENT MAKE A LIST OF THE EVIDENCE THEY ARE USING TO SUPPORT IT.
ORIGINAL DOCUMENTS
META-STUDY PUBLISHED IN REPU
JOURNAL
PHOTOGRAPH (SLIGHTLY
OPINION PIECE IN R
BOOK
FIELD
YOU CAN THEN CHECK THAT THE EVIDENCE THEY PRESENT IS ACCURATE BY SEEING IF IT IS INDEPENDENTLY CORROBORATED BY EXPERTS IN THE FIELD..
...IF IT'S NOT, CROSS IT OFF.
IF YOU ARE LEFT WITH A LONG AND CONVINCING LIST YOU SHOULD TAKE THE ARGUMENT MORE SERIOUSLY.
4
CHECK THE SOURCES OF THE SOURCES
WHEN YOU ARE READING THE SOURCES FOR ANY ARGUMENT CHECK WHO WROTE THEM AND CONSIDER ANY POTENTIAL VESTED INTERESTS THEY MIGHT HAVE.
I THINK WITH MY WALLET!
I THINK WITH MY HEART!
WHEN SOMEONE IS INVESTED IN AN IDEA THEY ARE MUCH MORE LIKELY TO FALL VICTIM TO BRAIN MISTAKES.
WHICH IS WHY GENERALLY ACADEMIC OR NON-PROFIT SOURCES OF INFORMATION ARE MORE LIKELY TO BE OBJECTIVE.
I THINK FOR MYSELF (AND MY IDEOLOGY)
5
SIMPLIFY
TO ENSURE YOU'RE NOT BEING TRICKED BY CLEVER RHETORIC OR DISTRACTED BY SOPHISTICATED LANGUAGE TRY REITERATING AN ARGUMENT IN SIMPLE TERMS.
THIS CAN OFTEN REVEAL GAPS IN LOGIC THAT HAVE BEEN BRUSHED OVER POETICALLY.
WHEN YOU HAVE TO CHOOSE BETWEEN TWO OR MORE EXPLANATIONS FOR SOMETHING A GOOD HEURISTIC IS OCCAM'S RAZOR WHICH STATES:
AMONG COMPETING HYPOTHESES, THE ONE WITH THE FEWEST ASSUMPTIONS SHOULD BE SELECTED.
WILLAM OF OCKHAM
OCCAM'S RAZOR
OR- THE SIMPLEST ANSWER IS USUALLY THE RIGHT ONE.

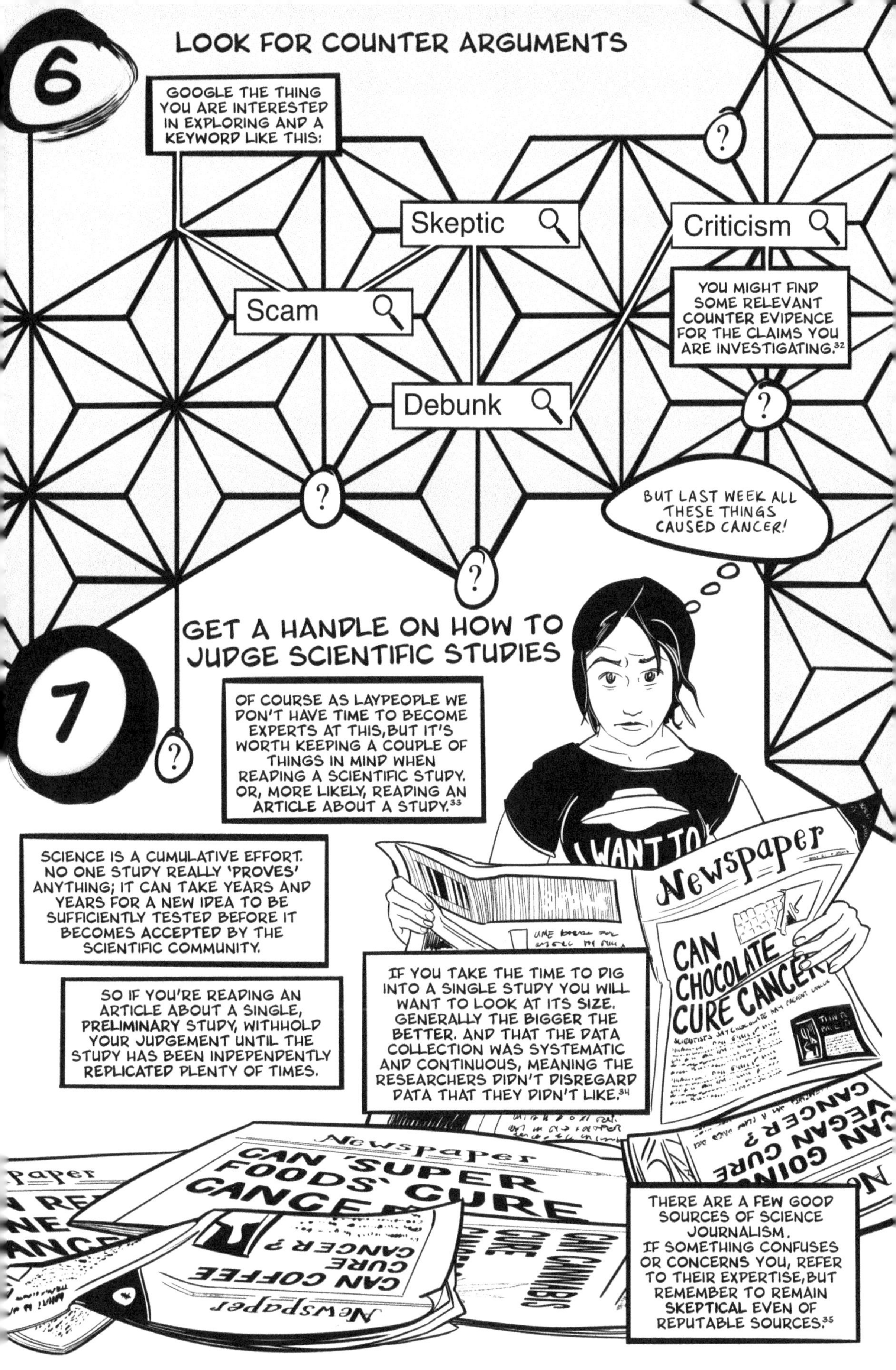

6
LOOK FOR COUNTER ARGUMENTS
GOOGLE THE THING YOU ARE INTERESTED IN EXPLORING AND A KEYWORD LIKE THIS:
Skeptic
Criticism
Scam
Debunk
YOU MIGHT FIND SOME RELEVANT COUNTER EVIDENCE FOR THE CLAIMS YOU ARE INVESTIGATING.[32]
BUT LAST WEEK ALL THESE THINGS CAUSED CANCER!
7
GET A HANDLE ON HOW TO JUDGE SCIENTIFIC STUDIES
OF COURSE AS LAYPEOPLE WE DON'T HAVE TIME TO BECOME EXPERTS AT THIS, BUT IT'S WORTH KEEPING A COUPLE OF THINGS IN MIND WHEN READING A SCIENTIFIC STUDY. OR, MORE LIKELY, READING AN ARTICLE ABOUT A STUDY.[33]
I WANT TO
Newspaper
CAN CHOCOLATE CURE CANCER
SCIENCE IS A CUMULATIVE EFFORT. NO ONE STUDY REALLY 'PROVES' ANYTHING; IT CAN TAKE YEARS AND YEARS FOR A NEW IDEA TO BE SUFFICIENTLY TESTED BEFORE IT BECOMES ACCEPTED BY THE SCIENTIFIC COMMUNITY.
SO IF YOU'RE READING AN ARTICLE ABOUT A SINGLE, PRELIMINARY STUDY, WITHHOLD YOUR JUDGEMENT UNTIL THE STUDY HAS BEEN INDEPENDENTLY REPLICATED PLENTY OF TIMES.
IF YOU TAKE THE TIME TO DIG INTO A SINGLE STUDY YOU WILL WANT TO LOOK AT ITS SIZE. GENERALLY THE BIGGER THE BETTER. AND THAT THE DATA COLLECTION WAS SYSTEMATIC AND CONTINUOUS, MEANING THE RESEARCHERS DIDN'T DISREGARD DATA THAT THEY DIDN'T LIKE.[34]
Newspaper
CAN 'SUPER FOODS' CURE
CAN COFFEE CURE CANCER?
CAN GOING VEGAN CURE CANCER?
CAN CANNABIS CURE
THERE ARE A FEW GOOD SOURCES OF SCIENCE JOURNALISM. IF SOMETHING CONFUSES OR CONCERNS YOU, REFER TO THEIR EXPERTISE, BUT REMEMBER TO REMAIN SKEPTICAL EVEN OF REPUTABLE SOURCES.[35]

8
LOOK FOR BIASES
YOU MIGHT FIND SOME CLASSIC BRAIN MISTAKES AND BIASES REPRESENTED BY THE PESKY CATS ALL OVER THIS PAGE!
WHEN MY BATTERIES RUN OUT, BAD THINGS HAPPEN...
OF COURSE IT WASN'T ME! LOOK HOW CUTE I IS!
ALL THE BIASES AND BRAIN MISTAKES I MENTIONED BEFORE AND MANY MORE COULD BE INFLUENCING WHOEVER IS MAKING THE CLAIM OR ARGUMENT THAT YOU ARE EXPLORING - ESPECIALLY IF THEY'RE INVESTED IN THE IDEA.
ALTHOUGH THE SCIENTIFIC METHOD IS DESIGNED TO TRY AND REMOVE THE EFFECT OF HUMAN BIASES, SCIENTISTS ARE NOT EXEMPT. FAMILIARISE YOURSELF WITH COGNITIVE BIASES AND WATCH OUT FOR THEM.
BUT...
...DON'T FORGET YOUR OWN BIASES!
ARE YOU ACCIDENTALLY SABOTAGING YOUR OWN RESEARCH BY ONLY SEARCHING FOR THINGS THAT CONFIRM YOUR BELIEFS?
WOAH! THE ODDS MUST BE CRAZY!
!
!
OR MAYBE YOU ARE READING WIDELY, BUT FINDING EXCUSES TO DISMISS PERSPECTIVES YOU DON'T LIKE, AND NOT QUESTIONING THOSE THAT YOU DO?
EVEN WHEN WE ARE DOING OUR BEST TO BE OBJECTIVE WE MAKE MISTAKES. WHICH IS WHY WE NEED TO REGULARLY PAUSE AND CONSIDER WHETHER WE MIGHT BE LETTING OUR BIASES CLOUD OUR REASONING.

9
PAY ATTENTION TO HOW YOU FEEL
"SKEPTICISM ISN'T ABOUT DENYING YOUR EMOTIONS, IT'S ABOUT UNDERSTANDING THEM."
- STEVEN NOVELLA[36]
SO, THERE USED TO BE THESE THINGS CALLED PHOTOGRAPHS, BUT THEY WERE PRINTED ON PIECES OF PAPER! AND YOU COULD GET THEM TAKEN IN SMALL BOOTHS, WITH A CAMERA INSIDE, AND THEY'D TAKE FOUR PICTURES, WITH ONLY A FEW SECONDS IN-BETWEEN, THEN PRINT THEM OUT ON A STRIP OF GLOSSY PAPER. YOU COULD DO A SERIOUS FACE IN THE FIRST TWO, TO USE FOR I.D., THEN HAVE FUN WITH THE THIRD AND FOURTH FLASH.
IF, WHEN YOU READ SOMETHING, IT MAKES YOU FEEL SUSPICIOUS THEN FOLLOW THAT LEAD - LOOK INTO IT!
BUT IF IT MAKES YOU HAPPY, SAD OR ANGRY THAT'S ALSO A GREAT INDICATOR THAT IT'S WORTH RESEARCHING FURTHER.
WE FEEL EMOTIONAL WHEN THINGS ARE IMPORTANT TO US AND WHEN THINGS ARE IMPORTANT TO US IT'S VITAL THAT WE FIGURE OUT THE TRUTH.
SKEPTICISM IS THE BEST WAY WE HAVE TO DO THAT.
I WANT TO BELIEVE
I WANT TO BASE MY BELIEFS ON REASON AND EVIDENCE
THE MORE YOU PRACTICE THIS SORT OF RIGOROUS SELF INQUIRY THE EASIER AND MORE HABITUAL IT GETS.
THE TRICK IS TO SWITCH THE WAY YOU THINK ABOUT YOURSELF FROM 'I AM A PERSON WHO BELIEVES IN X' TO 'I AM A PERSON WHO TRIES TO BASE MY BELIEFS ON REASON AND EVIDENCE'.
THIS DECREASES THE RESISTANCE TO CHALLENGING YOUR IDEAS AND MAKES YOU A MORE REASONABLE PERSON.

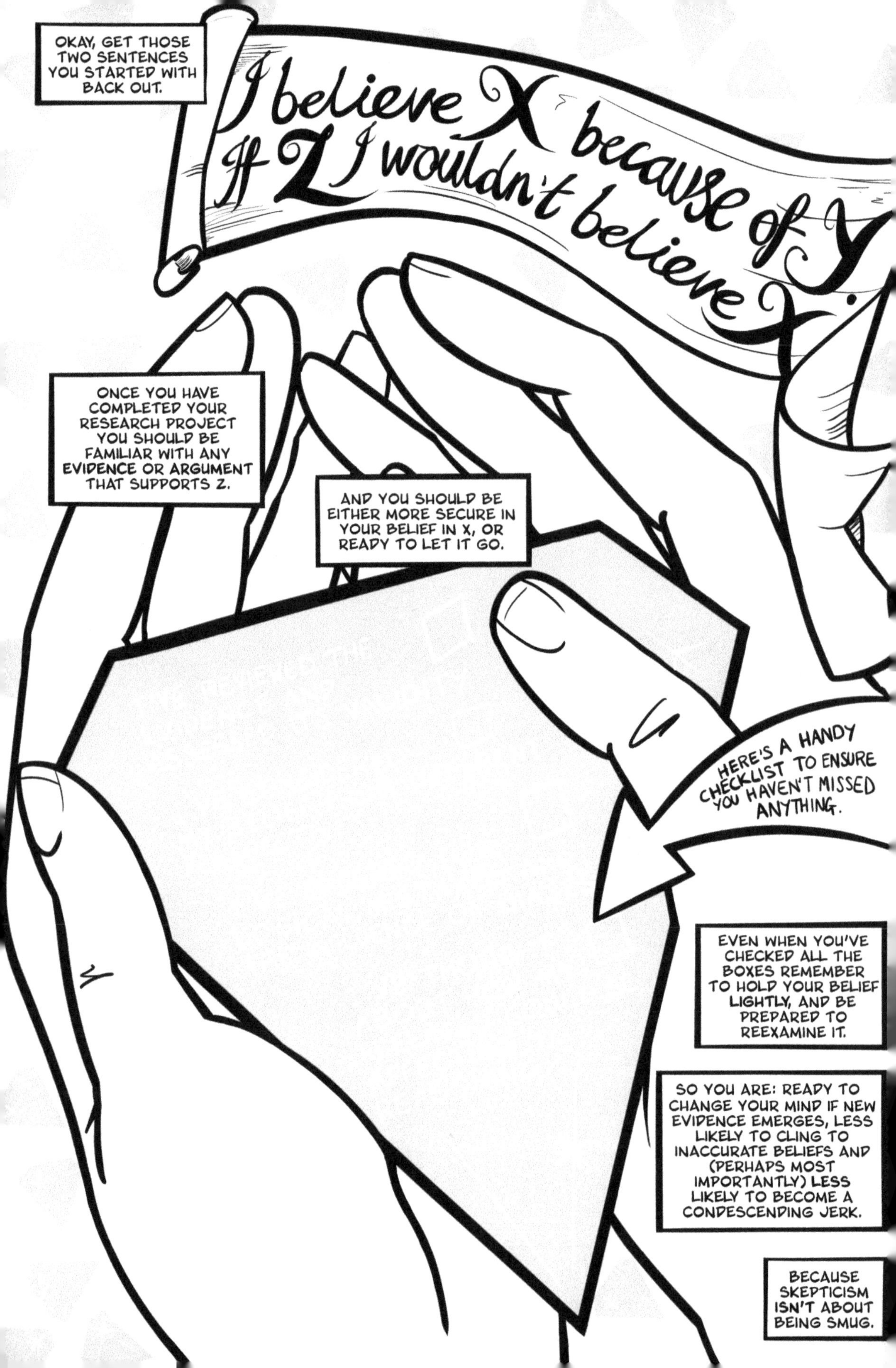
OKAY, GET THOSE TWO SENTENCES YOU STARTED WITH BACK OUT.
I believe X because of Y.
If Z I wouldn't believe X.
ONCE YOU HAVE COMPLETED YOUR RESEARCH PROJECT YOU SHOULD BE FAMILIAR WITH ANY EVIDENCE OR ARGUMENT THAT SUPPORTS Z.
AND YOU SHOULD BE EITHER MORE SECURE IN YOUR BELIEF IN X, OR READY TO LET IT GO.
HERE'S A HANDY CHECKLIST TO ENSURE YOU HAVEN'T MISSED ANYTHING.
EVEN WHEN YOU'VE CHECKED ALL THE BOXES REMEMBER TO HOLD YOUR BELIEF LIGHTLY, AND BE PREPARED TO REEXAMINE IT.
SO YOU ARE: READY TO CHANGE YOUR MIND IF NEW EVIDENCE EMERGES, LESS LIKELY TO CLING TO INACCURATE BELIEFS AND (PERHAPS MOST IMPORTANTLY) LESS LIKELY TO BECOME A CONDESCENDING JERK.
BECAUSE SKEPTICISM ISN'T ABOUT BEING SMUG.

THERE IS SO MUCH MISINFORMATION OUT THERE...
...AND AS IF THE WORLD WASN'T CONFUSING ENOUGH THERE ARE PLENTY OF PEOPLE READY TO DUPE US OUT OF OUR MONEY, OUR VOTE OR OUR FEALTY.[37]
BASE MY BELIEFS ON REASON AND EVIDENCE
UNFORTUNATELY THEY DON'T ALL LOOK LIKE ZOMBIES, OTHERWISE SPOTTING THEM WOULD BE MUCH EASIER.
SKEPTICS ARE DRIVEN BY A DUTY TO TRY AND PROTECT PEOPLE FROM MAKING MISTAKES AND FROM BEING EXPLOITED.

SKEPTICISM IS ABOUT TRYING TO MAKE THE WORLD A BETTER PLACE.
WHY DON'T WE TRY COMBINING THESE COMPOUNDS TO SEE IF W CAN DEVELOP A CURE?
NOT JUST BY PROTECTING OURSELVES AND OTHERS FROM SCAMS, BUT BY ASKING QUESTIONS THAT PROMOTE PROGRESS.
MAYBE WE COULD DO THIS IN COLOUR?

WHY ARE WOMEN TREATED AS SECOND CLASS CITIZENS?
BECAUSE NO PROGRESS, SCIENTIFIC, ARTISTIC OR ETHICAL, COMES WITHOUT DOUBTING THE STATUS QUO.
FOR WOMEN
VOTES

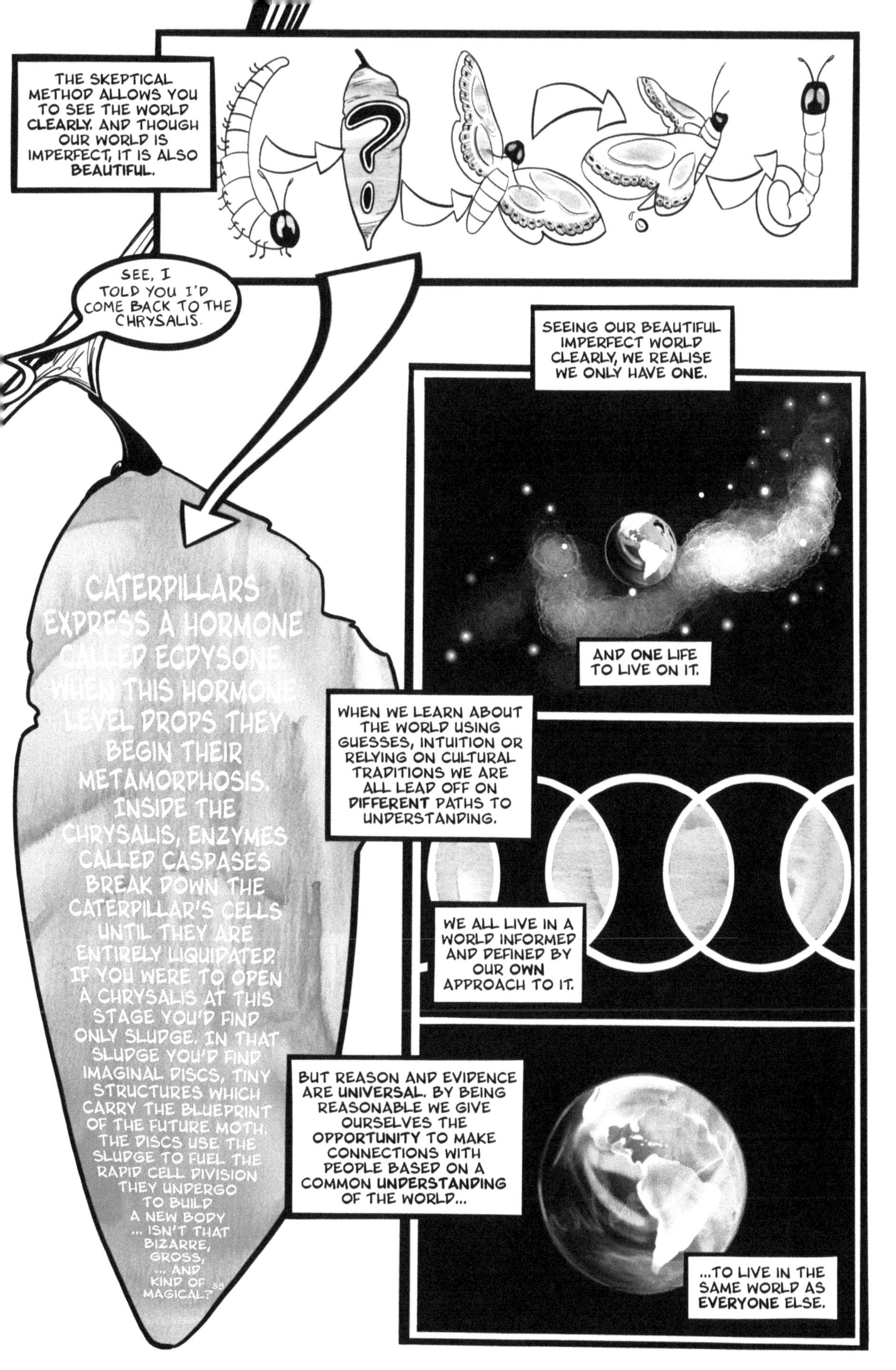
THE SKEPTICAL METHOD ALLOWS YOU TO SEE THE WORLD CLEARLY. AND THOUGH OUR WORLD IS IMPERFECT, IT IS ALSO BEAUTIFUL.
SEE, I TOLD YOU I'D COME BACK TO THE CHRYSALIS.
CATERPILLARS EXPRESS A HORMONE CALLED ECDYSONE. WHEN THIS HORMONE LEVEL DROPS THEY BEGIN THEIR METAMORPHOSIS. INSIDE THE CHRYSALIS, ENZYMES CALLED CASPASES BREAK DOWN THE CATERPILLAR'S CELLS UNTIL THEY ARE ENTIRELY LIQUIDATED. IF YOU WERE TO OPEN A CHRYSALIS AT THIS STAGE YOU'D FIND ONLY SLUDGE. IN THAT SLUDGE YOU'D FIND IMAGINAL DISCS, TINY STRUCTURES WHICH CARRY THE BLUEPRINT OF THE FUTURE MOTH. THE DISCS USE THE SLUDGE TO FUEL THE RAPID CELL DIVISION THEY UNDERGO TO BUILD A NEW BODY ... ISN'T THAT BIZARRE, GROSS, ... AND KIND OF MAGICAL?[38]
SEEING OUR BEAUTIFUL IMPERFECT WORLD CLEARLY, WE REALISE WE ONLY HAVE ONE.
AND ONE LIFE TO LIVE ON IT.
WHEN WE LEARN ABOUT THE WORLD USING GUESSES, INTUITION OR RELYING ON CULTURAL TRADITIONS WE ARE ALL LEAD OFF ON DIFFERENT PATHS TO UNDERSTANDING.
WE ALL LIVE IN A WORLD INFORMED AND DEFINED BY OUR OWN APPROACH TO IT.
BUT REASON AND EVIDENCE ARE UNIVERSAL. BY BEING REASONABLE WE GIVE OURSELVES THE OPPORTUNITY TO MAKE CONNECTIONS WITH PEOPLE BASED ON A COMMON UNDERSTANDING OF THE WORLD...
...TO LIVE IN THE SAME WORLD AS EVERYONE ELSE.

I DON'T KNOW IF THIS IS TRUE FOR ALL SKEPTICS, BUT I THINK SKEPTICISM HAS MADE ME HAPPIER.[39]
I AM CERTAINLY SAFER NOW THAT I HAVE THE SKILLS TO IDENTIFY POTENTIALLY DANGEROUS MISTAKES.
I WANT TO BASE MY BELIEFS ON REASON AND EVIDENC
I AM MORE CONFIDENT IN MY IMPORTANT CHOICES KNOWING THEY ARE BASED ON FALSIFIABLE BELIEFS BACKED BY SOLID EVIDENCE...
...AND I AM LESS LIKELY TO BE DISTRAUGHT WHEN ONE OF MY BELIEFS GETS OVERTURNED.
I AM ALSO MORE COMPASSIONATE. MAYBE THAT'S A 'GETTING OLDER THING' MORE THAN A 'BECOMING MORE REASONABLE THING', BUT EITHER WAY I AM NOW MORE ABLE TO ACT ON MY COMPASSION BY MAKING RATIONAL CHOICES THAT HELP OTHERS.
SO EVEN IF YOU'RE NOT SOLD ON SKEPTICISM AS A METHOD TO MAKE THE WORLD A BETTER PLACE, MAYBE YOU'LL LIKE THIS POTENTIAL SIDE EFFECT: OCCASIONAL BOUTS OF CONTENTMENT.

THIS IS ME.
I AM STILL SURROUNDED BY ALL THE STUFF AND NONSENSE IN THE WORLD. WE ALL ARE.
BUT NOW I'M NOT LOST IN IT.
I WANT TO BASE MY BELIEFS ON REASON AND EVIDENCE
REFORM NOW
COSTA
"WE WISH TO PURSUE THE TRUTH NO MATTER WHERE IT LEADS. BUT TO FIND THE TRUTH, WE NEED IMAGINATION AND SKEPTICISM BOTH."
CARL SAGAN
CARL SAGAN (THAT'S HIM) DESCRIBED SCIENCE AS A CANDLE IN THE DARK...[40]

SKEPTICISM

FURTHER READING, LISTENING, WATCHING AND SOCIALISING

READ

The Demon Haunted World: Science as a Candle in the Dark. Astrophysicist and science communicator Carl Sagan's 1995 book intended to explain the scientific method to lay-people. Considered a key text by many skeptics.

Mistakes Were Made (But Not by Me): Why we Justify Foolish Beliefs, Bad Decisions, and Hurtful Acts. Social psychologists Carol Tavris and Elliot Aronson's 2007 book explores numerous cognitive biases and their impact in our political and personal lives.

Why People Believe Weird Things: Pseudoscience, Superstition and Other Confusions of Our Time. Renowned skeptic and editor of skeptic magazine Michael Shermer's 1997 book reflects on the psychology behind belief in the incredible.

What's the Harm? A website which documents the stories of people who have been harmed by lapses in critical thinking leading to financial loss, physical injury or death.
http://whatstheharm.net

LISTEN

Skeptics with a K. British fortnightly podcast. Each episode the irreverent hosts chat about current affairs and topics of perennial interest to skeptics.
http://merseysideskeptics.org.uk/podcasts

Skeptics' Guide to the Universe. American weekly podcast. Each episode the hosts skeptically examine several issues and present a game that allows listeners to hone their own critical thinking skills.
http://theskepticsguide.org

The Reality Check. Canadian weekly podcast. The hosts discuss topical 'controversies and curiosities' using critical thinking skills and wit to separate science-fact from science-fiction.
http://trcpodcast.com

Your Deceptive MInd: A Scientific Guide to Critical Thinking Skills. A 24 lecture course presented by professor Steven Novella, M.D. empowers students with knowledge and techniques which will improve their critical thinking skills. Available directly from The Great Courses or on Audible.com.

WATCH

Rethinking Doubt: The Values and Achievements of Skepticism. An impassioned TedX talk from prominent skeptic George Hrab which introduces the audience to skepticism and explains its critical importance. Available on the TEDx YouTube channel.

Captain Disillusion. A YouTube channel produced by independent filmmaker Alan Melikdjanian. In monthly installments The Captain humorously debunks viral videos.

James Randi Educational Foundation. A YouTube channel curated by the James Randi Educational Foundation featuring lectures from prominent skeptics on many topics.

MEET

Skeptics in the Pub. Informal meetups held all over the world predominantly in the U.K. and U.S. events usually feature a talk, a Q&A session and a chance to socialise with fellow skeptics.
http://skepticsinthepub.org

Your Local Skeptic Society. Try Googling your location and the word skeptic, most countries have at least one skeptical organisation that hosts social and educational events. You could also try looking for skeptically themed events on meetup.com.

NOTES

1 To learn more about why we believe the things we do I recommend Michael Shermer's 2011 book *The Believing Brain: From Ghosts and Gods to Politics and Conspiracies - How We Construct Beliefs and Reinforce Them as Truths.*

2 WhatsTheHarm.net is a website that documents the stories of people who suffer negative consequences due to lapses in critical thinking.

3 One of many conspiracy theories currently in vogue is that the clouds of condensed water that we see behind airplanes are actually toxic chemicals. A good website explaining the science behind this mistaken idea is ContrailScience.com.

4 Slenderman is a character created by Eric Knudsen on the website Creepy Pasta. For more background on Slenderman consult the website KnowYourMeme.com. On May 31st 2014 in Wisconsin two teenage girls who professed belief in Slenderman attacked another girl apparently at his behest. For a detailed discussion of the ideas behind the Slenderman meme I recommend an episode of the podcast *Monster Talk* entitled *Slenderman and Tulpas* (Jul 30, 2014).

5 The website Anti-VaccineBodyCount.com documents the number of people who have died of vaccine preventable illnesses since the start of the modern Anti-Vax movement in 2007. At time of writing (October 31, 2017) they have documented 9028 deaths. To understand why people make life-endangering choices based on health-related misinformation I recommend Sarah and Jack Gorman's 2017 book *Denying to the Grave: Why We Ignore the Facts That Will Save Us.*

6 Scams can be simple or complex and we are all potential victims. In her 2016 book *The Confidence Game: Why we Fall For it... Every Time* Maria Konnikova details some extraordinary examples and examines the psychology of both the con-artist and their mark.

7 To learn more about the many different flavours of snake oil currently on sale to people who need medicine I recommend Harriet Hall's ten lecture series *Science Based Medicine*. Available on the James Randi Foundation YouTube channel.

8 Despite there being no scientifically credible mechanism by which prayers or positive thinking could change people's lives, beyond providing comfort and equanimity, there have been some studies into the effectiveness of praying for health improvements. Wikipedia has a whole Studies on Intercessory Prayer page devoted to the literature. Meta-studies find no effect or a potential very small effect.

9 The skeptical movement is a distributed community of people who attempt to understand the world using reason and evidence. Wikipedia's Skeptical Movement page offers a good overview. To understand how the modern skepticism movement fits into the history of science and philosophy I recommend Daniel Loxton's 2014 talk *A Rare and Beautiful Thing*. Available on the James Randi Foundation YouTube channel.

10 To learn more about the various biases that affect human reasoning and their origins and effects I highly recommend Elliot Aronson and Carol Tavris' 2007 book *Mistakes Were Made (But Not by Me): Why We Justify Foolish Beliefs, Bad Decisions and Hurtful Acts.*

11 The scientific method is, simply put, a process of generating hypotheses, testing them and reaching conclusions. Wikipedia's Scientific Method page offers a good overview.

12 Many modern medicines are synthesised from compounds originally found in nature, rainforests are particularly rich sources of medicinal compounds. Chris Bird and Omar Sattaur's article for New Scientist *Medicines From the Rainforest* (August 17, 1991) discusses the many medicinal plants discovered in rainforests.

13 Genetically engineered, drought-resistant crops have the potential to save many lives in drought prone regions of the world. Genetic engineering of food crops has many other potential life saving applications such as fortifying wheat with vitamin D in areas where vitamin D deficiency is a major cause of infant blindness and simply producing more plentiful yields in regions where food is scarce. For more information about GMO crops consult the website GMOAnswers.com.

14 In his impassioned 2015 TEDx talk *Rethinking Doubt: The Value and Achievements of Skepticism* George Hrab stresses the importance of the skeptical movement focusing on the desire to protect people from dangerous misinformation. Available on the TEDx Talks YouTube channel.

15 Skeptic Magazine's Skeptical Activism webpage suggests some ways to get involved in Skeptical activism. Find it on Skeptic.com.

16 Once we have generated an answer to a question we are resistant to changing our mind or even reexamining the issue. To learn more about this phenomena and how our attempts to be reasonable are often self-sabotaged I recommend Dan Sperber and Hugo Mercier's 2017 book *The Enigma of Reason: A New Theory of Human Understanding.*

17 Wikipedia maintains a List of Cognitive Biases and a List of Fallacies, both are interesting but humbling (and very long) reads. Most of the 'brain mistakes' in this book can be found among them.

18 To understand how Confirmation Bias affects our lives and interacts with other biases I recommend Elliot Aronson and Carol Tavris' 2007 book *Mistakes Were Made (But Not by Me): Why We Justify Foolish Beliefs, Bad Decisions and Hurtful Acts.*

19 Wikipedia's Ad Hominem page offers a good overview of this commonly used informal fallacy.

20 If you're still unsure about how the maths works out there's a great video *23 and Football Birthdays* that explains 'the birthday problem'. Available on the Numberphile YouTube channel.

21 The fascinating blog *The Odds Must be Crazy!* examines seemingly bizarre chance events by deconstructing the mathematical probabilities of events. Find it at SkepticInk.com/tombc.

22 Wikipedia's Animal Slaughter page has a detailed breakdown of the number of animals by species killed per year in the animal agriculture industry. Fifty-six billion is a lowball estimate.

23 Malaria is one of the most prolific diseases known to man, and though it is preventable and treatable, still one of the biggest killers. For more details consult the World Health Organisation's 10 Facts on Malaria webpage on WHO.int.

24 If you are interested in finding out which charities are most effective at reducing suffering, AnimalCharityEvaluators.org and GiveWell.org have already done the hard work for you by analysing the efficacy of hundreds of charities working to help animals and people.

25 Effective Altruism is a movement devoted to identifying the most effective charities (that save the most amount of lives, or alleviate the most suffering, for the least amount of money) and encouraging people to donate to them. Find out more at: EffectiveAlturism.org.

26 Our tendency towards group-think has been documented extensively. To learn more I recommend Philip Fernbach and Steven Sloman's 2017 book *The Knowledge Illusion: Why We Never Think Alone*.

27 The Bigfoot breeding population would have to be huge to sustain the species existence. In a post on the SGU Science News blog *There Are 100,000 "Bigfoots" in North America* (October 23, 2014) Evan Bernstein discusses the discrepancy between a large population of large primates living in North America and the complete lack of physical evidence of their existence. Find it on TheSkepticsGuide.org.

28 When we are financially or emotionally invested in a belief or our identity is invested in an idea our resistance to changing our minds is heightened. This is an example of post hoc rationalisation; we justify our decisions and refuse to see their flaws especially when acknowledging our mistake will lose us money, upset us or make us look foolish. For more on post-hoc rationalisation Elliot Aronson and Carol Tavris' 2007 book *Mistakes Were Made (But Not by Me): Why We Justify Foolish Beliefs, Bad Decisions and Hurtful Acts.*

29 Philosopher of science Karl Popper popularised the concept of falsifiability in his 1934 book *The Logic of Scientific Discovery.*

30 Wikipedia is not considered a reliable source for academic research, but in comic books there are no rules! But seriously, although you shouldn't rely entirely on Wikipedia it has become an excellent resource. In an article for Wired Magazine *At 15 Wikipedia is Finally Finding it's Way to the Truth* (January 15, 2016) Cade Metz gives a brief history of Wikipedia and its increasing reliability. Find it on Wired.com.

31 Wikipedia's Occam's Razor page offers a good overview of this principle.

32 Skeptical activist Tamar Wilner has gathered a useful list of resources she calls *The Lasso of Truth* which will help you wade through the Google search results. Find the list on her website along with an archive of helpful blog articles on the subject of navigating information online at TamarWilner.wordpress.com.

33 For an overview of how to judge scientific data and which sources to trust I recommend Steven Novella's 10 lecture course *Your Deceptive Mind* available on Audible.com and TheGreatCourses.com.

34 Elisabeth Pain's article for Sciencemag.com *How to (seriously) Read a Scientific Paper* (March 21, 2015) is a great place to start if you are interested in digging into some studies.

35 In his great blog ScienceOrNot.net Graham Coghill provides guidance on reading science journalism with a skeptical eye.

36 This quote is from Steven Novella's excellent 10 lecture course *Your Deceptive Mind* available on Audible.com and TheGreatCourses.com.

37 WhatsTheHarm.net is a website that documents the stories of people who suffer negative consequences due to lapses in critical thinking. Often these people are victims of charlatans, con-artists or scammers who take advantage of our desperation and naivety.

38 More details on what gross/fascinating stuff goes on inside a chrysalis can be found in Ferris Jabr's article for ScientificAmerican.com *How Does a Caterpillar Turn into a Butterfly?* (10th of August 2012).

39 It's not just me that's noticed this correlation between happiness and good critical thinking skills. In his 2017 book *Weaponized Lies: How to Think Critically in the Post-truth Era* Daniel Levitin cites research that suggests people who engage in 'evidence based thinking' are likely to live longer, get better grades, exhibit greater degrees of conscientiousness, suffer from fewer health problems and experience more life satisfaction.

40 Carl Sagan's 1995 book *Demon Haunted World: Science as a Candle in the Dark* explains the scientific method for lay-people and is considered a key text by many skeptics. The quote comes from the first episode of Sagan's 1980's television series *Cosmos: A Personal Voyage.*

CPSIA information can be obtained
at www.ICGtesting.com
Printed in the USA
BVHW021401191020
591325BV00009B/1620

9 781910 780763